APPLES

A TRUE BOOK

by

Elaine Landau

Children's Press®

A Division of Grolier Publishing

New York London Hong Kong Sydney
Danbury, Connecticut

Peeling apples

Reading Consultant
Linda Cornwell
*Coordinator of School Quality
and Professional
Improvement, Indiana State
Teachers Association*

*Author's Dedication
For Jocelyn Kessler*

**Visit Children's Press® on the
Internet at:
http://publishing.grolier.com**

Library of Congress Cataloging-in-Publication Data

Landau, Elaine.
　　Apples / Elaine Landau.
　　　　p.　cm. — (A true book)
　　Includes bibliographical references and index.
　　Summary: Surveys the history, cultivation, and uses of apples and
describes the different kinds.
　　ISBN 0-516-21024-6　(lib.bdg.)　　0-516-26571-7　(pbk.)
　　1. Apples—Juvenile literature.　[1. Apples.]　I. Title.　II. Series.
SB363.L234　1999
634'.11—dc21　　　　　　　　　　　　　　　　　　98-47327
　　　　　　　　　　　　　　　　　　　　　　　　　　CIP
　　　　　　　　　　　　　　　　　　　　　　　　　　AC

GROLIER
PUBLISHING

Contents

Many orchards invite families
to pick their own apples.

Apples

Have you ever heard the saying, "An apple a day keeps the doctor away"?

Perhaps you felt special after being told, "You're the apple of my eye."

You probably know the phrase, "An apple for the teacher." Years ago children

Apple pie is a national favorite.

brought their teachers large, shiny apples as gifts.

It seems that apples have always been with us. After all, who hasn't heard the expression, "It's as American as apple pie."

Perhaps more than any other fruit, apples are a part of American life. About 260 million bushels of apples are grown in the United States each year. They are important to the country's economy.

Bushels of apples

The value of America's apples before they are shipped to stores is about 1.25 billion dollars.

In the United States the greatest numbers of apples are grown in Washington, Michigan, and New York. California, Pennsylvania, North Carolina, Virginia, and West Virginia also rank high in apple production. But if you think of apples as just an American fruit—think again.

Young apple trees in bloom

The United States is the world's second largest apple-producing nation. More apples are grown in China than anywhere else on earth. Other nations known for their apple production are Russia, France, Turkey, and Italy.

Various types of apples are
grown throughout the world.
Some kinds of apple trees
have thrived in Iran's heat.
Others have survived Siberia's
freezing temperatures. The
only continent apples aren't
grown on is Antarctica.

Apples Through the Ages

Every time you eat an apple you are actually carrying on a tradition. People have been eating apples for over two million years. The ancient Greeks and Romans took pride in the different types of apples they grew. And when

The ancient Greeks enjoyed apples.

Roman soldiers conquered new regions, apple trees were usually planted there as well.

The Romans brought apples to many parts of England. And much later, when English colonists set off for North America they took apple seeds and small trees with them.

Settlers from other European countries, such as Holland and Spain, came to America with apple trees and seeds as well.

Apples proved useful in several ways. Often they were eaten raw. But they were also used to make apple cider and

Apples being pressed for cider

apple butter. Apple cider was a common drink in colonial America. It was about as popular as soft drinks are today.

Settlers moving west as the country grew brought apple seeds with them. There are many stories about how apple orchards sprang up across the country. But one of the best-known ones is based on fact. It's the tale of Johnny Appleseed.

Johnny Appleseed's real name was John Chapman.

Johnny Appleseed's mission to plant apple trees has inspired many tales.

Born in 1774 in Massachusetts, Chapman headed west as a young man. Along the way he stopped to clear the land and plant apple seeds. Before moving on he would build a brush fence around each small orchard.

This protected the new trees from wild animals. Chapman came back every so often to check on the trees. Then he would sell or trade them to settlers coming into the area. The settlers saved the seeds from the best trees for replanting. The worst-tasting apples were fed to the pigs and other livestock.

Some say Johnny Appleseed used a tin pot for a hat. It's also been said that he traveled barefoot. There are many stories of his kindness to animals. And he supposedly was good friends with the American Indians. When settlers found apple trees plant- ed around Indian villages, some said Chapman had supplied the seeds. But no one knows for sure how much of this is true.

Nevertheless, it's certain that Johnny Appleseed planted trees in Pennsylvania, Ohio, and Indiana. Before he died in 1845, his apple orchards covered over 1,200 acres (486 hectares).

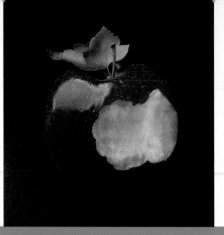

When you bite into an apple, you are perhaps enjoying the result of Johnny Appleseed's long-ago efforts.

None of Johnny Appleseed's trees are still alive. But trees grown from the seeds of his trees may still exist. Apples from these trees could be available at a supermarket near you. The next apple you bite into might just be one.

A Choice of Apples

Apples are good for you. Although they are 85 percent water, they contain vitamins A and C and potassium. Apples are also a good source of fiber, which aids in digestion. Eating fresh apples regularly may benefit your teeth and gums as well.

Apple Snacks

It's fun to prepare apples for after-school munching. With an adult's help, you can even cook a special apple dessert for company. Try these two recipes using your favorite variety of apple.

Apple Smiles

You will need:
- one red apple
- peanut butter (the kind without nuts)
- small marshmallows.

Cut the apple into slices—these will look like the lips. Spread peanut butter on one side of each apple, then stick three or four of the marshmallows in the peanut butter to make the teeth. These are silly but delicious!

Baked Cinnamon Apples

Have these ingredients ready:
- four baking apples
- four teaspoons of margarine,
- a half-cup of brown sugar
- a teaspoon of cinnamon.

Ask an adult to help you core (remove the seeds from) the apples. These become four apple cups for filling. Place these standing upright in a baking dish, and put two tablespoons of brown sugar, 1 teaspoon margarine and 1/4 teaspoon cinnamon in the center of each apple. Microwave for 6-8 minutes. Enjoy!

A crab
apple tree
in bloom

Thousands of different types of apples are grown through-out the world. There are also apples that grow in the wild. Many of these are crab apples. Crab apples are usually small and too sour to eat fresh. But some types are fine for canning and making applesauce, juice, wine, cider, and jelly.

Among the most popular kinds of apples cultivated (purposely grown) in the United States are:

Delicious apples: These dark red, oval-shaped apples are sweet and juicy. They are usually eaten fresh.

Golden Delicious: Like red Delicious apples, these are oval-shaped and sweetly flavored.

Red Delicious apples

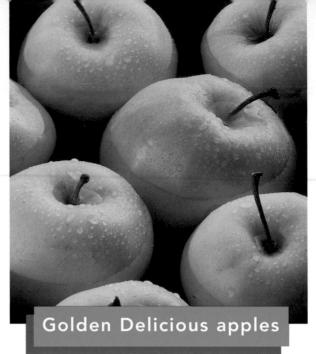
Golden Delicious apples

Such apples are often eaten
fresh or baked in pies.

Granny Smith: These near-
ly round, bright green apples
are firm and tart, or sharp
tasting. Granny Smith apples
can be eaten fresh or cooked
for various dishes.

24

A Granny Smith apple

McIntosh apples

McIntosh: The McIntosh is a bright red, medium-size apple that tastes sweet to mildly tangy. McIntosh apples are generally eaten fresh. But they are also used for applesauce.

Rome Beauty: These large, crisp red apples are mostly used for cooking and baking. Often they are cored and filled with nuts and raisins before placed in the oven to bake.

Cortland: Cortland apples are tender, juicy, dark red apples with a sweet to tangy flavor. They may be eaten fresh but are especially great in fruit salad. That's because their white flesh does not turn brown as quickly as many other kinds of apples.

Winesap: Winesap apples are dark red and round. They are both eaten fresh and used for apple cider.

Cox's Orange Pippins: Known for their orange yellow color, these apples are extremely well liked in England.

Cox's Pippin apples in an English orchard

Growing Apples

Apple trees come in different sizes. Some grow to about 40 feet (12 meters)—the height of a medium-size office building. Others are small enough to fit in your living room.

You could try to plant an apple tree from the seeds of an apple you enjoyed. And a

Apple trees can reach towering heights.

tree might grow and bear fruit. But you might not like its apples. They probably would not be as large or tasty as the one you took the seeds from.

Apple growers guard against this by not using seeds. Instead they use a process called grafting. First they cut a shoot, known as a scion, from a tree with fruit they like. The scion is grafted or attached to a rootstock.

Rootstocks are tree stems with roots that have been specially prepared for this process. The rootstock is cut open and the scion is fixed to it. Wax is poured over the cut portion to protect it from insects. The scion and rootstock join together to form a new apple tree.

Apple growers have grafted two kinds of apple tree varieties (left), then (right) poured protective wax over their work.

You can also get quality apples using a bud graft. A bud, which is also called a scion, is cut from a tree with good apples. The bud is placed inside a slit in the bark of a rootstock.

This orchard farmer is checking grafted seedlings.

The bud and rootstock are then wrapped together to grow into a new tree. With either type of grafting, the new tree's fruit will be like the ones the shoots or buds were taken from.

Naturally, this doesn't happen all at once. A tree gives fruit three to five years following grafting. First small flower buds appear. The buds blossom into lovely pink and white flowers called apple blossoms.

Apple blossoms decorate the orchard in spring.

You may be surprised to learn that each flower is the start of an apple. The flower's pretty color and sweet fragrance (smell) draw birds and insects to it. Honey bees are especially helpful here.

They fly to the flower to collect its nectar. Nectar is the thick sweet fluid within the flower. Bees use nectar to make honey. But as the bees take the nectar, pollen grains from the flower often stick to

Honey bees play an important role in the apple growing business.

their bodies. When these bees fly to a different tree's blossoms—the pollen drops off on other flowers.

The pollen fertilizes the flower. Later on its petals will fall off. But the green part of the flower that remains will grow into an apple. As it becomes rounded and riper, it will look more and more like the fruit. And by the time it's ready to be picked it will have become the proper color.

However, during this process, the tree and its fruit must be protected from insect pests. Growers spray their trees with chemicals called pesticides. These kill the insects that attack the trees.

Spraying pesticides by tractor (left) and helicopter (bottom)

But traces of pesticides can remain on the apple. That's why it's important to thoroughly wash any apples you eat.

Fruit growers fight insect pests in other ways as well. Sometimes they'll bring in other insects that feed on those which damage the trees. Growers are also trying to create new types of apples which appeal less to these harmful pests.

From Tree to Table

Apples are usually harvested by summer's end or in early fall. The greatest number of apples are picked in October. Not surprisingly, October has been declared National Apple Month.

Dessert apples (those eaten fresh) are picked by hand. This is to make sure that they won't

By autumn the trees are loaded with ripe apples for picking (left). An apple harvest worker (right) picks Granny Smiths for market.

be bruised or damaged in any way. On tall trees ladders may be needed. But some growers have large numbers of small, or dwarf, apple trees. It's easier to reach the fruit on these. Such trees also take up less space in an orchard.

Apples used for juice, cider, apple butter, applesauce, vinegar, and other products are picked by machines. Then all the apples are placed in bins and kept in cold storage. Afterward they are usually washed and placed on a moving

Larger orchards use mechanical harvesters.

rubber belt, called a conveyor belt, to dry.

Frequently, the apples are sorted according to size while on the belt. Small to medium-size apples are put in plastic bags for delivery to stores. Dessert apples may be individually wrapped in paper and placed on cardboard trays or in boxes.

Some apples are sold in markets immediately. But every year about a quarter of the United States' apples are preserved in cold storage. There temperatures are cold enough to keep the fruit fresh for twelve months. This allows us to enjoy great tasting apples year round.

Although apples store well, they taste best right off the tree.

To Find Out More

Here are some additional resources to help you learn more about apples:

 **Books**

Burckhardt, Ann. **Apples.** Bridgestone Books, 1996.

Dorros, Arthur. **A Tree Is Growing.** Scholastic Press, 1997.

Dowden, Anne Ophelia Todd. **From Flower To Fruit.** Ticknor & Fields, 1994.

Holland, Gini. **Johnny Appleseed.** Raintree Steck-Vaughn, 1997.

Maestro, Betsy. **How Do Apples Grow?** HarperCollins, 1992.

Robin, Fay. **We Love Fruit.** Children's Press, 1992.

Organizations and Online Sites

Apples and More
http://www.urbanext.uiuc. edu/apples/

Apple stories, history, nutrition, festivals, and facts.

Fruit and Vegetable Encyclopedia: Apples
http://www.dole5aday.com/ encyclopedia/apple/apple__ menu.html#menu

Crossword fun, nutrition news, tips for picking, storing, and eating apples.

The Johnny Appleseed Home Page
http://www.msccornell.edu/ 967Eweed/schoolpages/ appleseed/welcome/html

Interesting facts and amazing stories about the legendary John Chapman.

U.S. Apple Association
6707 Old Dominion Drive
Suite 320
McLean, VA 22101-1137
http://www.usapple.org

Trade association for the U.S. apple industry. Visit the U.S. Apple Store and the News Room, learn "Core Facts" and "Juicy Apple Stories."

Washington Apple Commission
2900 Euclid Avenue
Wenatchee, WA
98807-0018
http://www.bestapples.com/

Send a postcard, enter a contest, and learn everything there is to know about Washington apples.

Important Words

annual yearly

continent one of the earth's seven great bodies of land

cultivate to grow

digestion the process of breaking down food in the body

fragrance a pleasant smell or odor

grafting the process of joining parts from two trees to make a single tree

livestock farm animals

nectar a thick, sweet fluid from flowers

pesticide a chemical used to destroy insect pests

rootstock a stem with roots

scion a shoot or bud cut from a tree

tart a sharp, sour taste

thrive to grow or prosper

46

Index

Meet the Author

Elaine Landau worked as a newspaper reporter, an editor, and a youth services librarian before becoming a full-time writer. She has written more than one hundred nonfiction books for young people, including True Books on dinosaurs, animals, countries, and food.

Ms. Landau, who has a bachelor's degree in English and journalism from New York University and a master's degree in library and information science from Pratt Institute, lives in Florida with her husband and son.